Il Barbiere di Siviglia.
(The Barber of Seville.)
Overture.

Nº 1. "Piano, pianissimo.„
Introduction.

Time of the action, near dawn; place, an open square in Seville. At the left the house of Bartolo, its windows having practicable bars and closed blinds, which can be unlocked and locked at the proper time. Fiorello, lantern in hand, ushers in a number of musicians with their instruments. Later, Count Almaviva, wrapped in a cloak.

Fiorello. (coming forward cautiously)

Pia - no, pia - nis - si - mo, sen - za par - lar,
Hush, let us soft - ly tread, breathe not a word,

tut - ti con me ve - ni - te qua, ve - ni - te qua.
No one must see, no one must see, no one must hear.

No 2. "Ecco ridente in cielo.„
Cavatina.

Ec - co ri - den - te in cie - - lo spun - ta la bel - la au -
Dawn, with her ro - sy man - - tle, Stands at the gate __ of

ro - - ra, e tu non sor - gi an - co - - ra, e ____
morn - ing, Night's gloom a - far is driv - - en, Yet ____

Nº 3. Continuation and Stretta of Introduction.

Count.

il gior-no a-van-za.
is far ad-vanc-ing.

Ah che pen-so!
Yet she stirs not!

cresc.

f

che fa-rò?
All is vain___

pizz.

Tut-to è va-no—
I'll dis-miss them:

p

p stacc.

Buo-na gen-te!—
Friends, come hith-er,

Chorus (sotto voce).

A-
Come

Mio si-gnor—
Sir, we come.

(The Count gives his purse to Fiorello, who distributes money to the musicians.)

van-ti, a-van-ti!
nearer, come nearer!

Più di suo-ni, più di
Here I need no more de-

p

can-ti,
tain ye,

più di suo-ni, io bi-so-gno or-mai non
Take my thanks, yes, my good friends, take my thanks and

Fiorello.

ho. Buona notte a tut-ti quanti, più di voi che far non sò, buo-na
go. Here no longer we will de-tain ye, So good-bye, my friends, now go, Here no

notte, buo-na not-te, più di voi che far non sò.
longer we'll de-tain ye, So good-bye, my friends, now go.

(The musicians surround the Count, thanking him and kissing his hands and the hem of his cloak; he, annoyed

Allegro vivace.
Vlns. & Fag.

by their noisy demonstrations, tries to chase them off, as does also Fiorello.)

Count.

Ba-sta,
Silence,

Chorus.

Mil-le grazie, mio si - gno-re, del fa - vo - re, del-l'o-
Sir, we humbly thank your ho-nor, No-ble pa-tron, gen'rous

det-ti, via di qua, via di qua, via di qua!
gone, ye servile herd, servile herd, servile herd!

det-ti, via di qua, via di qua, via di qua!
up-roar ev-er heard, ev-er heard, ev-er heard!

tà, qua-li - tà, qua-li - tà, qua-li - tà!
word, 'pon my word, 'pon my word, 'pon my word!

(exeunt musicians)

dim.

p

morendo

Recitative.

Count.   Fiorello.

Gen-te indiscre-ta! Ah qua - si con quel chiasso impor - tu-no, tut-to quan-to il quar-
Tur - bulent fellows! I thought they'd never end their noisy chatter, all the neighbors are

Count (looking towards the balcony).

tie-re han ri-sve-glia-to. Al-fin so-no par-ti - ti! E non si ve-de! E i-nu-ti -le spe-
stirring to know the reason. At last we have dispatch'd them. I cannot see her! I linger here in

mai quest'im-por-tu - no? La - scia-mo-lo pas-sar;   sot - to quegl' ar - chi non ve -
can be this in-trud-er? I'll hide and let him pass;   Un - der those arch-es none will

(Hides under the portico)

du-to, ve - drò quan-to bi - so-gna; già l'al-ba ap-pa - re, e a-mor non si ver-gogna.
see me, from thence I can observe him; 'tis now broad day-light, but love is never weary.

Nº 4. "Largo al factotum della città."
Cavatina.

Allegro vivace.

gior-no sempre d'in - tor - no   in gi-ro sta. Mi-glior cuc - ca-gna per un bar-
quire me, Nothing can tire me, rea-dy for all. Of all pro - fessions that can be

bie - re, vi - ta più no - bi - le, no, non si dà. La le ran la le ran la le ran
mentioned, That of a bar-ber is best of them all. La le ran la le ran la le ran

Fag. & Strings

la le ran la le ran la le ran la le ran la
la le ran la le ran la le ran la le ran la.

Ra - so - ri e   pet - ti - ni, lan-cet-te e
Scissors in   hand,'mongst my combs and my

for - bi - ci al mio co - man - do tut-to qui sta, lancet-te e   for - bi - ci, ra - so - ri e
ra - zors, I stand at the door, when customers call, Scissors in   hand,'mongst my combs and my

pet - ti - ni al mio co - man - do tut - to qui sta. V'è la ri -
ra - zors, I stand at the door when cus - tomers call. Then there are

sorsa poi del me - stiere col - la don - net - ta, col ca - va -
cases, quite di - plo - matic, Here damsel sigh - ing, there swain ec -

lie - re, col - la don - net - ta, la le ran le rà, cól ca - va - lie - re, la le ran
sta - tic, here damsel sighing, la le ran le ra, there swain ec - sta - tic, la le ran

la, la, la. Ah che bel vi - ve - re,
la, la, la. 'Tis a de - lightful life,

che bel pia - ce - re, che bel pia - ce - re per un bar - bie - re di qua - li -
brim - ful of plea - sure, brim - ful of pleasure, That of a bar - ber, used to high

ruc - ca, pre - sto la bar - ba, presto il bi - gliet - to! Fi - ga - ro, Fi - ga - ro,
wig there," "Quick here and shave me," "Run with this let - ter." Fi - garo, Fi - garo,

Fi - ga - ro, Fi - ga - ro, Fi - ga - ro, Fi - ga - ro, Fi - ga - ro, Fi - ga - ro, Fi - ga - ro Ahi - mè! ahi -
Fi - garo, Fi - garo, Fi - garo, Fi - garo, Fi - garo, Fi - garo, Fi - garo No more, no

mè! che fu - ria! ahi - mè! che fol - la! U - no al - la vol - ta
more! this cla - mor I'll bear no lon - ger! For pi - ty's sake, speak

per ca - ri - tà, per ca - ri - tà, per ca - ri - tà! u - no al - la
one at a time, for pi - ty's sake, for pi - ty's sake, for pi - ty's

vol - ta, u - no alla vol - ta, u - no al - la vol - ta per ca - ri - tà!
sake, speak one at a time, oh for pi - ty's sake, speak one at a time!

tà,— del - la__ cit tà,__ del — la__ cit tà, del - la cit -
town,— of__ all__ the__ town, of__ all__ the__ town, of all the

tà!
town!

Recit.

Figaro.

Ah, ah! che bel-la vi-ta! Fa-ti-car poco, di-vertirsi as-sa - i, e in tasca sempre a-
Yes, yes, this life is glorious! Not much to do, and plenty of a-musement, and always a dou-

ver qualche do-blo-ne. Gran frut-to del-la mia ri-pu-ta - zio-ne. Ec-co qua: senza
bloon with-in my pocket! The fruit of my exalt-ed re-pu - ta-tion. It is thus: without

Fi - garo non si ac-ca-sa in Si - viglia u-na ra-gaz-za; a me la ve-do-vel-la ri-
Fi - garo, not a girl in all Seville can find a husband; to me the gentle wi-dow turns

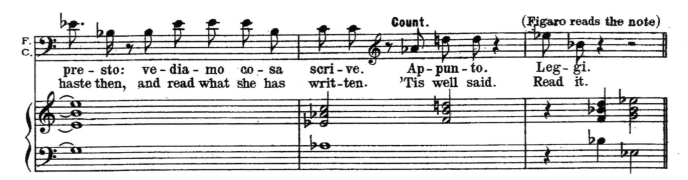

"Le vostre assidue premure hanno eccitata la mia curiosità. Il mio tutore è per uscire di casa; appena si sarà allontanato, procurate con qualche mezzo ingegnoso d'indicarmi il vostro nome, il vostro stato, e le vostre intenzioni. Io non posso giammai comparire al balcone, senza l'indivisibile compagnia del mio tiranno. Siate però certo, che tutto è disposta a fare, per rompere le sue catene, la sventurata Rosina."	"Your assiduous attentions have attracted my notice. My guardian is going out; as soon as he is gone, contrive some means to let me know your name, your condition and your intentions. I can never appear at the balcony without my inevitable tyrant; be assured, however, that every effort will be made to break her chains by the unfortunate Rosina."

Bartolo (talking toward the house)

iu-to! Che? S'a-pre la por-ta. Fra momenti io tor-no, non a-pri-te a nes-
by there! Why? The door is op'ning. Mind my orders, and mark me, not a soul here shall

(locking the house-door)

su-no. Se Don Ba-si-lio ve-nis-se a ri-cer-car-mi, che a-spet-ti. Le mie noz-ze con
enter but Don Ba-si-lio; should he come, you can tell him to a-wait me. Now my mar-riage with

(exit)

lei me-glio è affret-ta-re. Sì, den-tr'og-gi fi-nir vo' que-st'af-fa-re.
her must be conclud-ed; Yes, and af-ter, she need not be se-clud-ed.

Recitative.

Dentr'og-gi le sue noz-ze con Ro-si-na! Ah vec-chio rim-bam-bi-to! Ma
The marriage between him and my Ro-si-na! Ah, dotard most be-sotted! But

Figaro.

dimmi or tu: chi è que-sto Don Ba-si-lio? È un so-len-ne imbroglion di ma-tri-
tell me at once, who is this Don Ba-si-lio? Full of craft and intrigue, a sneaking

mo-ni, un col-lo tor-to, un ve-ro di-spe-ra-to, sempre sen-za un quat-tri-no_
scoundrel, maker of matches, a hy-pocrite accomplish'd, always short of three farthings,

F. ti-ro, os-ser-va-te: per bac-co, non mi sbaglio. Die-tro la ge-lo-si-a sta la ra-
moment, now look yonder; by Bacchus, I can see her. There, hid be-hind the curtains, stands your a-

F. gaz-za; pre-sto, presto all' as-sal-to, niun ci ve-de. In u-na canzo-net-ta co-sì al-la
dor'd one; now at once to the charge, sir, no one's looking. Now sing some little ballad, of your in-

F.
C.
F. buo-na il tut-to spie-ga-te-le, si-gnor. U-na can-zo-ne? Cer-to.
dit-ing, and tell her all you would have her know. I sing a bal-lad? Yes, sir.

Count. **Figaro.**

F.
C. Ec-co la chitar-ra, presto an-diamo. Ma i o— Oh che pa-zienza! Ebben, pro-via-mo.
Here, take my guitar then, quick, be-gin, sir. How can I? I lose all patience. I will convince her!

Count. **Figaro.** **Count.**

Nᵒ 5. Canzone.

Andante. *mezza voce*

C. Se il mio no-me sa-per voi bra-ma-te, dal mio
Who for e'er 'neath thy window is sigh-ing, Dost thou

Guitar & Strings pizz.

p

Nº 6. "Oh cielo! Nella stanza.„
Recit. and Duet.

№ 7. "Una voce poco fa.,,
Cavatina.

A room in the house of Dr. Bartolo. The windows closed with Venetian blinds. Rosina has a letter in her hand.

Andante

U - na vo - ce po-co fa qui nel cor mi ri - suo - nò, il mio
There's a voice that I en-shrine In my heart, and none must know; Ah, Lin-

rà,   e contenta io re-ste - rò. Sì, Lin - do - ro mio sa -
vine,   Till my hand I may be-stow. Yes, Lin - do - ro shall be -

rà, lo - giu - ra - i, la - vin - ce - rò, sì, Lin -
mine, I have sworn it, for weal or woe, Yes, Lin -

do - ro mio sa - rà, lo giu - ra - i, la vin - ce - rò!
do - ro shall be mine, I have sworn it, for weal or woe!

Moderato.

Rosina.

Sì, sì, la vin-ce-rò! Potessi al-me-no man-dar-gli que-sta let-te-ra. Ma
Yes, yes, I shall suc-ceed! If I could on-ly en-list a trust-y messenger. I've

co-me! Di nessun qui mi fi-do: il tu-to-re ha cent' occhi_ba-sta, ba-sta: si-gil-
no one, not a soul to con-fide in, I am watch'd by an Argus_Oh it's frightful! All the

(goes to the writing-table and seals the letter.)

lia_mo-la in-tan-to. Con Fi-ga-ro il bar-bier dal-la fi-ne-stra di-
same, I will seal it. With Fi-ga-ro he was there; I saw them talk-ing quite

scor-rer l'ho ve-du-to più d'un' o-ra. Fi-ga-ro e un ga-lant-uo-mo, un giovin di buon
plea-sant-ly toget-her in the morning. Fi-ga-ro might do something; he's civ-il and o-

Figaro.

co-re; chi sa ch'ei non pro-teg-ga il nostro a-mo-re! Oh, buon dì, Si-gno-
bliging. I'll see if I can get him to take this let-ter. Oh, good day, my young

Rosina. **Figaro.** **Rosina.** **Figaro.**

rina. Buon gior-no, signor Fi-ga-ro. Eb-be-ne? che si fa? Si muor di no-ia. Oh
lady. Good morning, Señor Fi-ga-ro. How say you? what's a-miss? I'm out of spirits. Im-

No. 8. "La calunnia è un venticello."
Recitative and Aria.

Recitative.

Basilio. Ah! che ne di-te? **Bartolo.** Eh! sa-rà ver, ma in-tan-to si per-de tem-po, e qui
Well, your opin-ion? Ah, I don't know; but meanwhile, the time is pressing, let us

strin-ge il bi-so-gno. No: vo' fa-re a mo-do mi-o; in mia ca-me-ra an-
have no more talk-ing. No, my own plan is the saf-est; we can set-tle it at

diam. Vo-glio che in-sie-me il con-trat-to di noz-ze o-ra sten-dia-mo. Quan-do sa-rà mia
once. Let us to-gether go and draw up the contract this ver-y in-stant. When I am once her

mo-glie, da que-sti zer-bi-not-ti in-na-mo-ra-ti met-ter-la in sal-vo sa-rà pen-sier
hus-band, I soon shall put a stop to her flir-ta-tions and ma-chi-na-tions. I know how to

Basilio. (They enter the first door R.H.)
mi-o. (Ven-gan da-na-ri: al re-sto son qua i-o)
rule her. (Con-ceit-ed do-tard! not e-ven how to school her!)

Nº 9. "Dunque io son."
Recit. and Duet.

Figaro (coming forward cau-tiously)
Voice. F.
Ma bra-vi! ma be-no-ne! ho in-te-so tut-to. Ev-vi-va il buon Dot-to-re!
How lucky that I heard them! All's fair in war-time. Long live our val-iant Doctor!

Piano.

F.
R. trat - to col ma - e - stro di mu - si - ca là den-tro s'è ser - ra - to. Sì? oh
in there, and Ba-si - lio, his coun-sel-lor, is drawing up the contract. Yes? is

Rosina.

R. l'ha sba-glia-ta a af - fè! po - ve - ro scioc-co! l'a - vrà da far con me. Ma di - te, si - gnor
that their pre-sent plan? we'll not dis-turb them, they'll find their match in me. Now tell me, Se - ñor

R. Fi - ga - ro, voi po-co fa sot - to le mie fi - ne-stre par - la - va-te a un si-gno - re?
Fi - ga - ro, a while a - go, just un-derneath my window, you were talk-ing to some one?

Figaro.

F. Ah, un mio cu - gi - no. Un bra-vo gio-vi - not-to; buo-na te - sta, ot - ti-mo cor; qui
Yes, it was my cou-sin, a young man of some promise, full of spir-its, excellent heart; just

Rosina.

F.
R. ven - ne i suoi stu-di a com-pi - re, e il po-ve-rin cer - ca di far for - tu - na. For-
now he is complet-ing his studies, and the poor boy thinks he will make his for-tune. His

Figaro.

R.
F. tu - na? eh la fa - rà. Oh, ne du - bi-to as - sa - i: in con-fi-den-za ha un
for-tune? And so he will. Oh, of that I am doubt-ful; between ourselves now, he

R. lar,_____ che__ mi__ de - vi con - so - lar, sì, con - so -
F. nar?   chi   v'ar - ri - va, chi v'ar-ri-va.a indo - vi - nar, a.in - do - vi -

rest,____ ah,__ my__ heart is__ now   at__ rest, ah, yes, my
press'd,   none   their craft, no, none their craft has e'er ex-press'd, no,   none their

R. lar, sì,   con - so - lar, sì, con-so - lar!
F. nar, a.in - do - vi - nar, a.in-do-vi - nar?

heart, ah yes, my heart is now at   rest! (exit Figaro)
craft, no,   none their craft has e'er ex - press'd!

ff

Nº 10. "A un dottor della mia sorte."
Recit. and Aria.

Rosina.   Bartolo.

Voice. R.
B.

O - ra mi sen - to meglio: questo Fi-ga-ro è un bravo gio-vi-not-to. In som-ma, col - le
Now all my doubts are ended, and to Fi-ga-ro I ev-er shall be grateful. Come here, child, there's a

Piano.

p

B.

buo - ne, po-trei sa-pe - re   dal - la mia Ro - si - na che venne a far co - lui que-sta mat-
ques-tion that you must answer,   like a good Ro - si - na: What did the barber call a-bout this

Andante maestoso.

(1) **Bartolo.**

Recitative.

Rosina.

Bron-to-la quan-to vuo-i, chiu-di por-te e fi-ne-stre, io me ne ri-do; già di noi
Cease not to storm and bluster, bar the doors and the windows; I do not mind you. Such pet-ty

femmine al-la più mar-motta per a-guzzar l'inge-gno e far-la spi-ri-to-sa tutto a un tratto ba-sta
tyranny turns a woman's temper, and rouses e'en the feeblest with mother-wit and slyness to resistance when you

(exit) Bertha (enters).

chiu-der-la a chia-ve e il col-po è fat-to! Fi-no-ra in questa ca-me-ra mi parve di sen-
think you have cag'd her, she most defies you. I thought I heard a murmuring, a talking in this

tir un mor-mo-ri-o; sa-rà stato il tu-tor col-la pu-pil-la, non han o-ra di ben. Queste ra-
room; who can have been here? our young la-dy, no doubt; per-haps her guardian, always finding some fault. None of our

(a knocking is heard) Count. (outside) **Bertha.**

gaz-ze non la vo-glion ca-pir. Bat-to-no. A-pri-te! Ven-go! Ec-
servants ev-er an-swer the door. Who is that? With-in there! Com-ing! At-

ci! an-co-ra du-ra: quel ta-bac-co m'ha po-sto in se-pol-tu-ra.
tchee! how ve-ry teaz-ing! 'Tis the med'cine this morning brought on this sneezing.

Nº 11. "Ehi di casa, buona gente!„
Finale I.

Count (disguised as a cavalry soldier).

Ehi di ca - sa,   buo - na gente,   buo - na
Eh, with - in there! come good people!   Up, a-

gente,   ehi,   ehi di ca - sa,   ehi di ca - sa!   niun ri -
rouse ye! eh,   eh, with-in there, eh, with-in there, are ye

Bartolo.

sponde! ehi! Chi è co - stu-i? che brutta faccia? è ub-bri-
sleeping? Eh! Who may this be? An ug-ly fel-low! Scarcely

Count (insists on embracing him).

C. Qua!
There!
So-no anch'io dottor per cen-to,
Am not I of the profess-ion?
ma-nescalco al reg-gi-
I'm the re-giment's phy-

C. men-to.
si-cian,
(presenting a paper)
Dell' al-log-gio sul bi-gliet-to, dell' al-log-gio sul bi-
And 'tis up-on you I'm quarter'd, and 'tis up-on you I'm

a piacere

C. gliet-to, os-ser-va-te, ec-co-lo qua, ec-co-lo qua, ec-co-lo qua, ec-co-lo qua.
quarter'd, read this or-der, it is quite true, it is quite true, it is quitetrue, it is quite true.

col canto

C. (Ah, ve-nis-se il ca-ro og-get-to
(Ah, how weary this pro-ba-tion!

Bartolo.

B. (Dal-la rab-bia, dal di-spetto io già cre-po in ve-ri-
(What with scorn and in-dig-nation, I know scarcely what to

p a tempo

Str. & Cor.

Wood

C. del - la mia fe-li-ci-tà!
Fair - est, bless my long-ing view.

B. tà.
do.
Ah, ch'io fo, se mi ci metto,qual-che gran be-stia-li-
I'm a man of moder-a-tion, Not a braw-ler such as

Nº 11ª "Fredda ed immobile.,,

Sestet from Finale I.

(He motions the Guard back, takes the Officer aside and shows him a paper. The Officer is astonished, orders the Guard to retire to the back, where he places himself at their head. All stand in amazement.)

Nº 11ᵇ "Ma signor."
Stretta from Finale I.

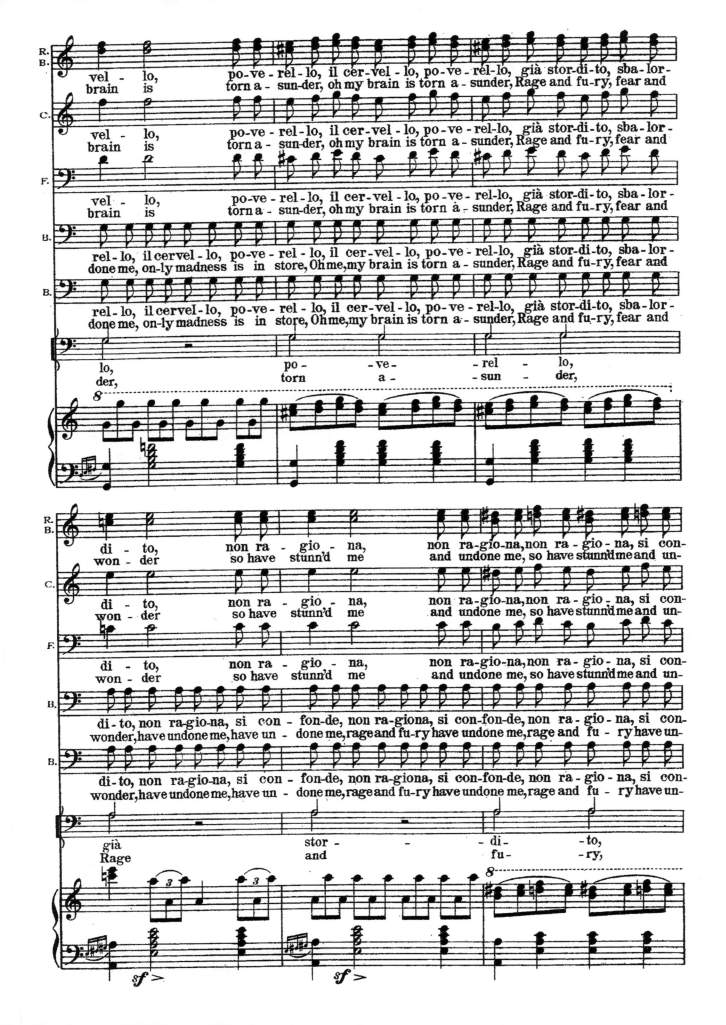

182

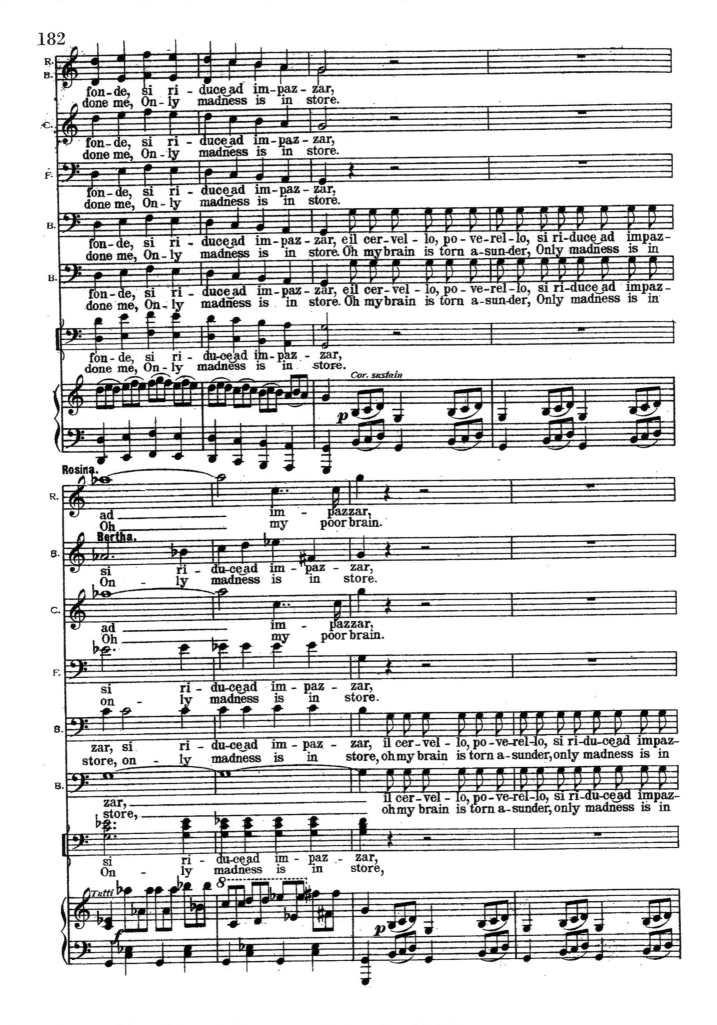

End of Act I.

Nº 12. "Pace e gioia sia con voi.„

Recitative and Duettino.

Scene.—The Library at Doctor Bartolo's; there are chairs and a pianoforte, on which is some music.

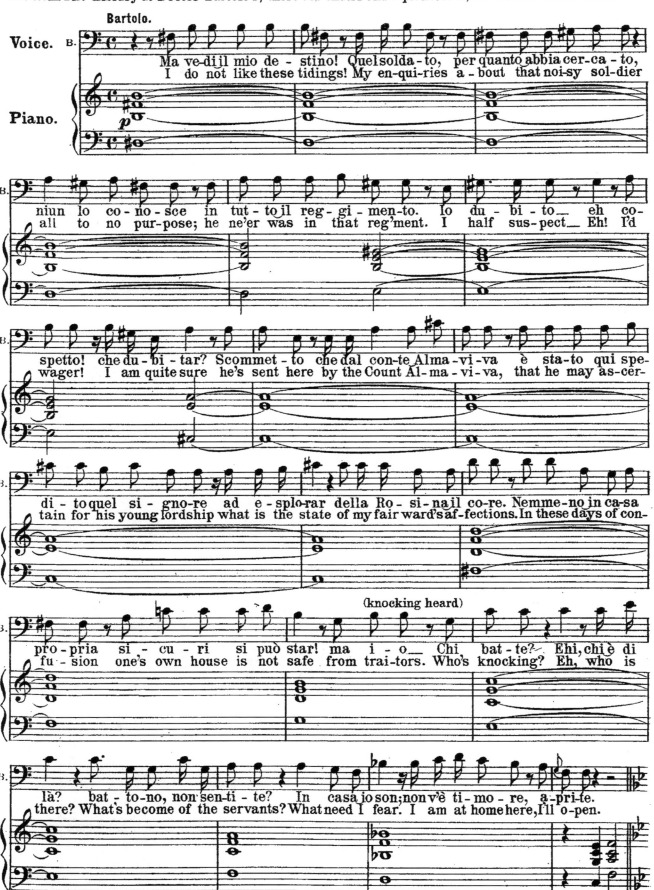

Recitative.

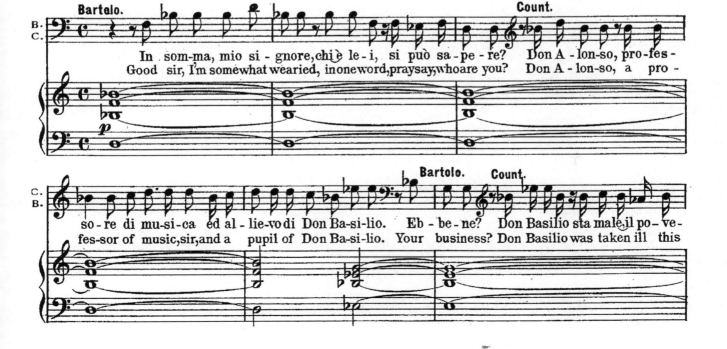

In som-ma, mio si-gnore, chi è le-i, si può sa-pe-re? Don A-lon-so, pro-fes-
Good sir, I'm somewhat wearied, in one word, pray say, who are you? Don A-lon-so, a pro-

so-re di mu-si-ca ed al-lie-vo di Don Ba-si-lio. Eb-be-ne? Don Basilio sta male, il po-ve-
fes-sor of music, sir, and a pupil of Don Ba-si-lio. Your business? Don Basilio was taken ill this

(showing a letter)

loggio, ed in mie ma-ni per ca-so ca-pi-tò que-sto bi-gliet-to del-la vo-stra pu-
vis-it, and by good fortune there fell in-to my hand the note you see here, from your niece to his

(taking the letter and looking at it)

Bartolo. Count.

pil-la à lui di-ret-to. Che ve-do! è sua scrit-tu-ra! Don Ba-si-lio nul-la sa di quel
lordship to his di-rection. This letter! it is her writing! Don Ba-si-lio does not know that I

fo-glio; ed io per lui ve-nen-do a dar le-zio-ne al-la ra-gazza vo-le-va far-me-ne un
found it, and as he wish'd that I should give the lesson to the lady, I had in-tend-ed that, en-

(seeking an excuse, he gets embarrassed)

Bartolo. Count.

me-ri-to con vo-i, per-chè con quel bi-gliet-to si po-treb-be Che co-sa? Vi di-
tire-ly for your int'rest, that she should see this let-ter, it might further Pray what, Sir? To be

rò, s'io po-tes-si par-la-re al-la ra-gaz-za, io cre-der-ver-bi-gra-zia le fa-
plain, if you will but per-mit me to see the la-dy, I think that with submission with this

re-i che me lo diè del con-te un' al-tra a-man-te; pro-va si-gni-fi-can-te, che il
let-ter, 'tis ea-sy to per-suade her the Count is faithless. He, with some oth-er mistress, might

Bartolo.

C.
B.

con-te di Ro-si-na si fa gio-co, e per-ciò— Pia-no un po-co. U-na ca-lunnia! Oh
careless-ly have left it where I found it, and perhaps— Well i-magined. But this is sland'ring. Oh

(embraces him, and puts the letter in his pocket)

B.

bra-vo! degno e ve-ro sco-lar di Don Basilio! Io sa-prò co-me me-ri-ta ri-com-pen-
bra-vo! I re-cognize the school of Don Basilio. Be as-sured of my gra-ti-tude for all you

B.

sar sì bel sug-ge-ri-men-to. Vo'a chia-mar la ra-gaz-za, poi-chè tan-to per
do, and for your good in-tentions. I will call the young la-dy. Since I know that to

B.
C.

me v'in-te-res-sa-te, mi rac-co-man-do a vo-i. Non du-bi-ta-te.
me you're so de-vot-ed, in friendship pray com-mand me. I'm your's de-vot-ed.

Count.

(Bartolo enters an inner room)

C.

L'af-fa-re del bi-gliet-to dal-la boc-ca m'è u-sci-to non vo-len-do. Ma co-me
This sto-ry of the let-ter quite a-gainst my in-ten-tion has es-caped me; what could I

C.

far? Sen-za un tal ri-pie-go mi toc-ca-va andar vi-a co-me un baggia-no. Il
do? But for some such pre-text he would soon have ex-pell'd me as a preten-der. My

Recitative.

 rò. Che vo - le - te cantar? Io can-to, se le aggra-da, il Rondò dell' "I - nu-til Precau-
gin. And what song shall it be? If you have no ob - jec-tion, I will sing something from the "Vain Pre-

zione.„ Eh sem-pre, sempre in bocca "L'i-nu-til Pre-cau-zio-ne!„ Io ve l'ho det-to: è il
caution.„ That's what she's always saying; what is this "Vain Pre-caution?„ Have I not told you, an

ti-to-lo del - l'o-pe-ra no-vel-la. Or be-ne, in-te-si: an-dia-mo.
o-pe-ra that's ev-ry-where per-form'd now. Well, well, then, I hear you, be-gin now.

Rosina. Count. (the Count seats himself at the pianoforte; Bartolo takes a seat and listens)

Ec - co-lo qua. Da bra-va! in - co - min - cia-mo.
Here is the air. Al - low me, let us be - gin then.

№ 13. "Contro un cor che accende amore.„
Aria.

Rosina. (sings to the Count's accompaniment)

Con-tro un
When a

cor che ac -cen-de a -mo-re di ve - ra - ce in-vit - -to ar-
heart with love is glowing, Love that's last-ing, de-vo - tion o'er-

do- - re, s'ar - ma in-
flow- - -ing, 'Tis in

van po- -ter ti - -ran- - -no di ri-
vain you would op- -press it, 'Tis in

rà, giu - bi - le - rà.
fail, will nev - er fail.

Moderato.

Rosina.

Ca - ra im - ma - gi - ne_ ri - den - te, dol - ce i
Yes,_ my_ heart, in thee con - fid - ing, Now_ with_

de - a d'un lie - to a - mor, tu_ m'ac - cen - di
hope and joy_ is_ blest; Thee I_ trust_

in pet - to il co - re, tu mi por - tia de - li - rar, tu mi
with faith a - bid - ing, Ev -'ry_ care_ is lull'd to_ rest, ev -'ry_

Nº 14. "Quando mi sei vicina."
Recitative and Arietta.

Recitative.

Bartolo. (perceiving Figaro.)   **Figaro.**

Bra - vo, si - gnor bar - bie - re, ma bra - vo!   Eh nien - te af - fat - to: scu - si, son de - bo -
Nice man - ners for a bar - ber! go on, sir!   Oh pray ex - cuse me, real - ly, I did not

Bartolo.   **Figaro.**

lez - ze. Eb - ben, gui - do - ne, che vie - ni a fa - re? Oh bel - la! ven - go a
mean it. You rogue, come tell me, what do you come for? I come for? why what

Bartolo.   **Figaro.**

far - vi la bar - ba: og - gi vi toc - ca. Og - gi non vo - glio. Og - gi non vuol? Do-
else but to shave you? this is your day, sir. This day I can - not. This day you can't? I'm

Bartolo. **Figaro.** (puts his basin on a table, and takes a memorandum - book out of his pocket.)

ma - ni non po - trò i - o. Per - chè? Perchè ho da fa - re, a tut - ti gli Uf - fi - zia - li del
sor - ry, to - mor - row I can't. Why not? Because to - mor - row I must at - tend the reg²ment, their

nuo - vo reg - gi - men - to, bar - ba e te - sta, al - la mar - che - sa Androni - ca il bion - do par - ruc-
beards will all want dressing, be - sides their shav - ing; then there is the old Marchioness who just has sent her

chin coi ma - ro - nè; al con - ti - no Bom - bè il ciuf - fo a cam - pa - ni - le; pur-
wig for me to dress; then the young Count Bom - bè has sent to have his hair curl'd; then

gan-te al-l' av-vo-ca - to Ber-nar - do - ne, che ie - ri s'am-ma - lò d'in-di-ge-stio-ne_ e
med²cine for the law-yer Ber-nar - do - ne, who's just been tak-en ill of in-di-ges -tion; be-

(replacing the book in his pocket)

Bartolo.

poi, e po - i, che ser - ve? do-man non pos - so. Or - sù, me-no pa-
sides some oth-ers, to-mor-row's full of en - gagements. Well, well, no more of

Figaro.

ro - le. Og - gi non vo' far bar - ba. No? co-spet - to, guar-da-te che av-ven-
talk-ing. This day you shall not shave me. Oh, in -deed, sir? This is a pret - ty

to - ri! ven-go sta-ma-ne; in ca-sa v'è l'in-fer-no; ri-tor-no do-po
house-hold! I call this morn-ing, find ev -'ry-thing in up-roar; this af-ter-noon re-

(imitating Bartolo)

pran - zo: og - gi non vo - glio. Ma che! m'a-ve-te pre - so per un qual-che bar-
turn-ing, "I won't be shav'd now." For what, sir, do you take me? for some bar-ber of

(taking up his basin as though about to go)

Bartolo.

bier da con-ta-di - ni? Chia-ma-te pur un al-tro, i - o me ne va-do. Che
naught, up from the coun-try? Pray get your-self an-oth-er; no more will I serve you. What

No 15. "Don Basilio! Cosa veggo!"
Quintet.

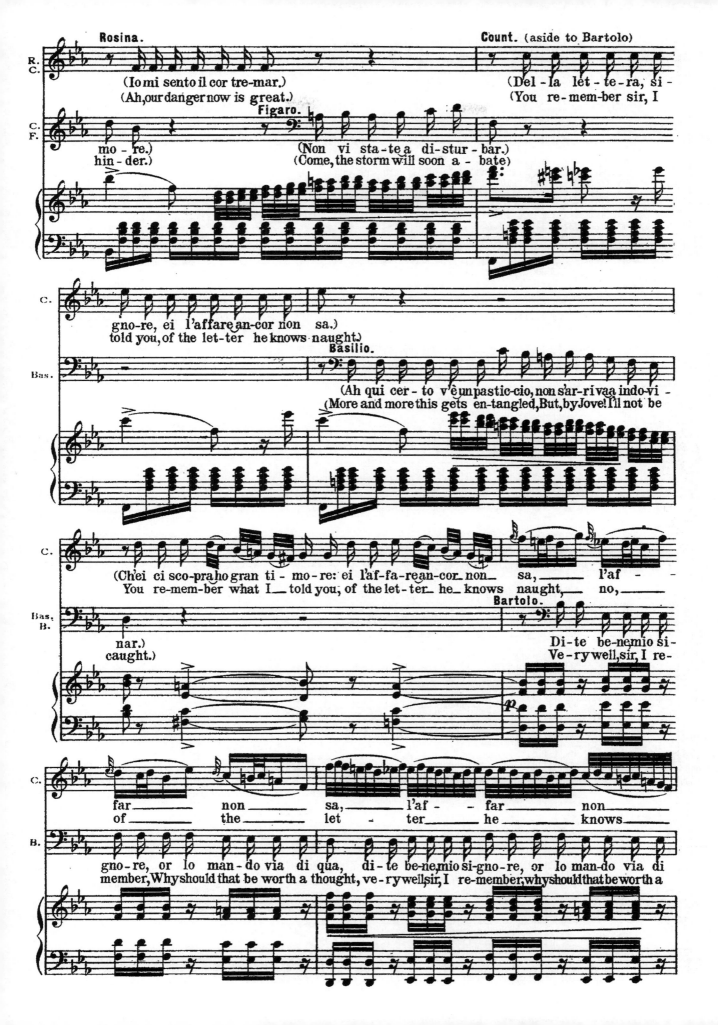

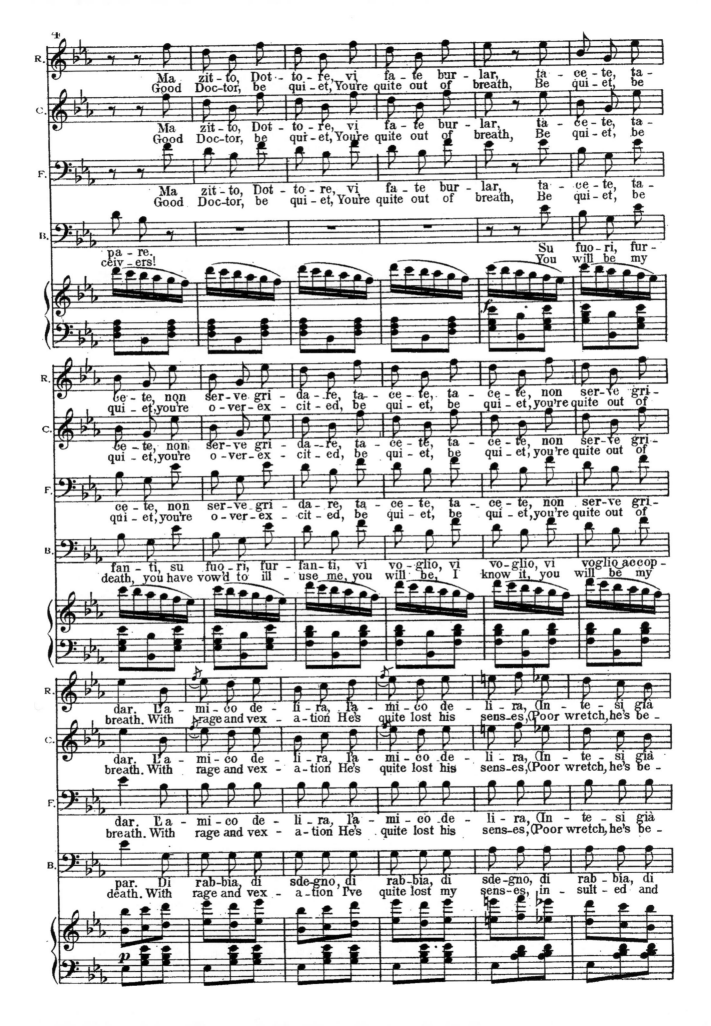

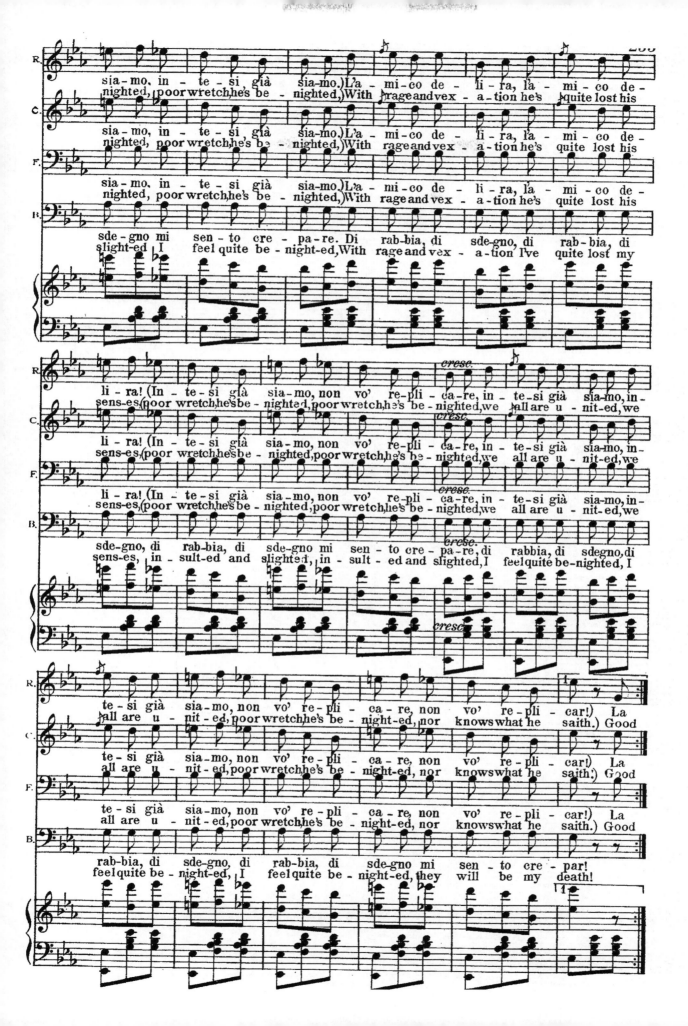

"Ah! disgraziato me!„
Recitative.

due son da le - gar!
self-same way are mad!

Ma che co - sa è que-sta-
What's the cause of this con-

mo - re,
fu - sion?

che fa tut - ti de - li - rar?
What's this love, that makes them mad?

Ma che co - sa è que-sta - mo-re,
What's the cause of this con - fusion?

che fa
What's this

tut - ti de - li - rar? Egli è un ma-le u-ni-ver - sa-le, u - na smania un piz-zi-
love, that makes them mad? The com-plaint is u - ni - ver-sal, Tis a glamour, an il-

a piacere

co - re, u - na sma-nia un piz-zi - co-re, un sol - le-ti-co, un tor-men-to. Po-ve-
lu-sion,'tis a glamour, an il - lu-sion,'Tis a crav-ing, what can heal it? I my-

cresc.

mi con - vien co - sì cre - par,
there's no com - fort to be had,

mi __ con - vien co -
there's no __ com - fort

sì cre-par, co - sì cre - par, co - sì cre - par,
to be had, no, there's no com - fort to be had,

ff

mi con - vien co - sì __ cre - par!
there's no __ com-fort __ to be __ had!

(Exit.)

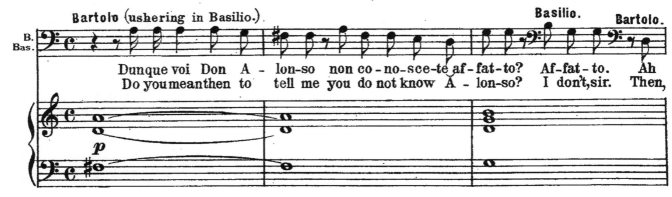

"Dunque voi Don Alonso non conoscete affatto?„

Recitative.

Room with barred windows, as in the first Act.

Bartolo (ushering in Basilio.)   Basilio.   Bartolo.

Dunque voi Don A - lon-so non co - no - sce-te af - fat - to? Af - fat - to. Ah
Do you mean then to tell me you do not know A - lon-so? I don't, sir. Then,

p

cer - to, il Con-te lo mandò. Qualche gran tra-di-men - to si prepa-ra. Io poi di-co che quell'a.
doubtless he's sent here by the Count. Be assur'd that some scheme's in preparation. And I tell you that Don A.

Basilio.

mi-co e - ra il Con-te in per-so-na. Il Con-te? Il Con-te. (La bor-sa par-la
lon-so is the Count himself in person. You think so? I know it. (The purse told me dis-

Bartolo. **Basilio.**

Bartolo.

chia-ro.) Sia chi si vuo-le, a-mi-co, dal No-ta-ro vo' in que-sto pun-to an-
tinctly.) Well, if it were so, the need is all the great-er at once to call the

da-re; in que-sta se-ra sti-pu-lar di mie noz-ze io vo' il con-tratto. Il No-tar? sie-te
lawyer; this ver-y evening he must come and draw up the contract of my marriage. What? to-night? are you

Basilio.

mat-to? pio-ve a tor-ren-ti, e po-i que-sta se-ra il No-ta-ro e impe-
cra-zy? rain pours in tor-rents; besides, too, I was told that this evening he has

Bartolo.

gna-to con Fi-ga-ro; il bar-bie-re ma-ri-ta sua ni-po-te. U-na ni-po-te? Che ni-
bus'ness with Fi-ga-ro, for the barber bestows his niece in marriage. His niece in marriage? You are

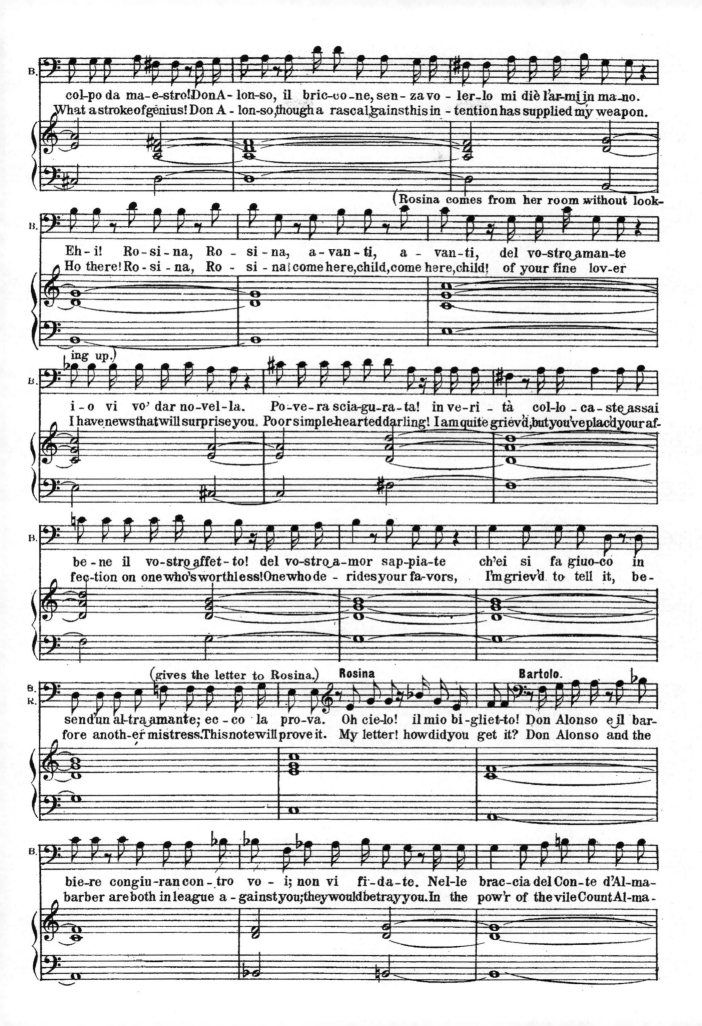

col-po da ma-e-stro! Don A-lon-so, il bric-co-ne, sen-za vo-ler-lo mi diè l'ar-mi in ma-no.
What a stroke of genius! Don A-lon-so, though a rascal 'gainst his in-tention has supplied my weapon.

(Rosina comes from her room without look-

Eh- i! Ro-si-na, Ro-si-na, a-van-ti, a-van-ti, del vo-stro aman-te
Ho there! Ro-si-na, Ro-si-na! come here, child, come here, child! of your fine lov-er

ing up.)

i- o vi vo' dar no-vel-la. Po-ve-ra scia-gu-ra-ta! in ve-ri-tà col-lo-ca-ste assai
I have news that will surprise you. Poor simple-hearted darling! I am quite griev'd, but you've plac'd your af-

be-ne il vo-stro affet-to! del vo-stro a-mor sap-pia-te ch'ei si fa giuo-co in
fec-tion on one who's worthless! One who de-rides your fa-vors, I'm griev'd to tell it, be-

(gives the letter to Rosina.) Rosina   Bartolo.

send un al-tra amante; ec-co la pro-va. Oh cie-lo! il mio bi-gliet-to! Don Alonso e il bar-
fore anoth-er mistress. This note will prove it. My letter! how did you get it? Don Alonso and the

bie-re congiu-ran con-tro vo-i; non vi fi-da-te. Nel-le brac-cia del Con-te d'Al-ma-
barber are both in league a-gainst you; they would betray you. In the pow'r of the vile Count Al-ma-

Rosina.

vi-va vi vo-glio-no con-dur-re. (In braccioa un al-tro! Che mai sen-to! ah Lin-
vi-va theyhave resolvedto place you. (Count Al-ma-vi-va! Can this be so? Oh Lin-

do-ro! ah tra-di-to-re! ah sì! ven-det-ta! e veg-ga, veggaquell'empiochi è Ro-
do-ro! Artthou a traitor? But I'll have vengeance! And teach thee, heartless betrayer, to know Ro-

Bartolo.

si-na.) Di-te Si-gno-re, di spo-sar-mi vo-i bra-ma-va-te. E il
si-na.) Tell me, good Doc-tor, do you still wish to be-come my hus-band? More than

Rosina.

vo-glio. Eb-ben, si fac-cia! i-o son con-ten-ta! ma al-l'i-
ev-er! I now con-sent, then; take me, I am will-ing; but on the

stan-te. U-di-te: a mezza not-te qui sa-rà l'in- de-gno con Fi-ga-ro il bar-
in-stant. I'll tell you: When it is midnight, he this roomwill en-ter, with Fi-ga-ro as

Bartolo.

bier; con lui fuggi-reper spo-sar-lo io vo-le-va. Ah scel-le-ra-ti! Cor-ro a sbarrar la porta.
well; all is arranged that then we fly from here together. Oh,band of scoundrels! I'll run the doorto fasten.

№ 17. Storm.

From the windows flashes of lightning are seen, and thunder is heard throughout this movement. When the storm subsides the shutters are opened from without, and Figaro, followed by the Count, enters by the window; they are both wrapped in cloaks, and Figaro carries a lantern.

No 18. "Ah qual colpo inaspettato.„
Recitative and Trio.

Voice. F. C.

Figaro.   Count.

Al - fi - ne   ec - co - ci   qua.   Fi - ga - ro, dammi man.   Po - ter del
One more step, and here we   are.   Fi - ga - ro, lend a hand! Great Father

Piano.   p

Figaro.   Count.

C. F.

mon - do! che tem - po in dia - vo - la - to!   Tempo   da innamo - ra - ti.   Ehi, fam - mi
Neptune, this night is down up - on us!   Ah, sir, 'tis lovers' weather. Come, strike a

C. lu - sa! oh me fe - li - ce! a - dunque tu di ve - ra - ce a - mo - re a - mi Lin -
lu - sion! hap - py im - pos - ture! Ro - si - na! say, dost thou love sincerely the poor Lin -

Rosina.   Count.

C.
R. dor? ri - spon - di! Ah sì! T'a - mai pur trop - po! Ah! non è
dor? Oh tell me. I do! I love him fond - ly! Ah! 'tis the

(he kneels before her, throwing off

C. tempo di più ce - lar - si; a - ni - ma mi - a: rav - vi - sa co - lui che sì gran
moment for my un - mask - ing. Turn, oh my sweetest, and lis - ten, be - hold thy fond a -

his cloak, which Figaro takes up)

C. tem - po se - guì tue trac - cie, che per te so - spi - ra, che sua ti vuo - le;
dor - er, him, who so long hath follow'd in thy foot - steps with true de - vo - tion;

C. mi - ra - mi, o mio mio te - so - ro, Al - ma - vi - va son i - o, non son Lin - do - ro!
Love was the sole deceiver, to thy heart I'm Lin - do - ro, else Al - ma - vi - va!

C.

F.

(Qual tri -
(Oh, she

ten-to. Guar-da, guarda il mio ta-len-to che bel col-po sep-pe far!)
pleasure! Henceforth Fi-ga-ro's at lei-sure, Having join'd the happy pair.)

C.

on — fo,   qual tri-on-fo i-na-spet-ta — to!   me fe-
loves___me!   oh what un-ex-ampled plea — sure!   My con-

C.

li — ce!   oh bel   mo — men — — to! Ah! d'a-
tent-ment   ex-ceeds   all mea — — sure, 'Tis__ my

C.

mo — re   e di con-ten — to   son vi-
own___now,   the__heart I__ trea — sure,   Joy-ful__

R.

ti - sti,   a - mor,   pie
dan - ger   we now____ de -

C.

ti - sti,   a - mor,____ pie
dan - ger   we now____ de -

F.

presto andiam, presto andiam, presto andiam per ca - ri - tà!
come a - way, come a - way, fly while yet there's time to fly!

Strings

R.

tà! Ah! _____
fy. Ah! _____

C.

tà!   Ah! _____
fy.   Ah! _____

R.

C.

Figaro.

F.

Ah! _____
Ah! _____

Fl.

"Ah disgraziati noi!„
Recitative.

Nº 19. "Cessa di più resistere."
Scene.

Bartolo.

Il Con-te! ah che mai sen-to! Ma co-spet-to!__ T'ac-che-ta; in-van t'a-do-pri, re-si-sti in-van. De' tuoi ri-go-ri in-sa-ni giun-se l'ul-ti-mo i-stan-te. In fac-cia al mon-do si di-chia-ro al-ta-men-te co-stei mia spo-sa: il no-stro no-do, o ca-ra,o-pra è d'a-mo-re. A-mor, che ti fe' mia con-sor-te,

The Count himself? oh a-mazement! but con-found it!__ Be si-lent; vain is re-sistance, your pow'r is gone. A base, designing tyrant, now your victim es-capes you. All these are witness, to the world I pro-claim her my wife, my countess. The tie that binds us is love unsought, un-fetter'd; henceforth,naught in life shall divide us;

rà,_____ più non tri - on - fe - rà!
pow'r,____ thy_ day_ of_ pow'r is__ o'er!

Andante. **Count.**

E tu, in - fe - li - ce vit - ti - ma d'un__
For - get now thy days of_ ty - ran - ny, Look__

reo po - ter__ ti - ran - no, sot - trat - ta al gio - go
up, my fair - est trea - sure, Let us en - joy in__

bar - ba - ro, can - gia in pia - cer_ l'af - fan - no, e in
li - ber - ty Long__ days of love and_ plea - sure! All

braccio, ve - ni - te qua, Dot - to - re. Ah noi fe - li - ci! Oh for - tu - nato a - mo - re!
brace me, come to my arms, good Doctor! Oh day of gladness! We shall be happy, my treasure!

Allegro.

Rosina. *Count.*

Figaro.

Di sì fe - li - ce in -
For - got is all re -

ne - sto ser - biam me - moria e - ter - na. Io smor - zo la lan -
sent - ment, The lov - ers are u - nit - ed, In fear and trouble

End of the Opera.

Aria

of

Don Bartolo,

by Pietro Romani.*)

English version by
Dr. Th. Baker.

*) This aria traditionally replaces Bartolo's music on pp. 110-123.

Allegro.

Ma   se poi per mia di - sgrazia voi la sor-da ancor fa -
But, if longer, to my   sorrow, you in e -vil ways per -

re-te,   le fi-ne-stre tro-ve-re-te si-gil-la-te e-ter-na-
sev-er,   Ev -'ry window, you'll dis-cover, shall be tightly barr'd for

men-te.   Farò incet-ta di chia-
ev-er.   I shall buy me keys in

vac-ci,   luc-chet-ti-ni e ca-te-nac-ci,
plen-ty,   Chains and pad-locks ten or twen-ty,

ser - ra - tu - re e chia-vi - stel-li, top-pe, chio-di, spranghe, e ar-
Lock the doors and bar the windows! Bolt you, bar you, nail you and

pio - ni, fa - ro in-cet - ta di chia vac - ci, luc - chet - ti e ca - te -
jail you! I shall buy me keys in plen-ty, Chains and pad-locks ten or

nac-ci, ser - ra - tu - re e chia-vi - stel-li, top-pe, chio-di, spranghe, ar-
twen-ty, Lock the door and bar the windows! Bolt you, bar you, nail you,

pio - ni: non son poi di quei bab-bio - ni che si
jail you! I'm no such old fool, I tell you, That you

fan-no in-fi-noc-chiar, di que' bab-bio-ni che si
ev - er can take me in! No fool, I tell you, That you

fan - no in - fi - chiar, non son poi di quei bab - bio - ni, non son poi di quei bab -
ev - er can take me_ in! I'm no such old fool, I tell you, I'm no such old fool, I

bio - ni che_ si fan - no in - fi - noc - chiar.
tell you, That you e'er can take me in!

Ma se poi per mia di - sgra - zia voi la sor - da ancor fa - re - te,
But, if long - er, to my sor - row, you in e - vil ways per - sev - er,

le fi - ne - stre tro - ve - re - te si - gil - la - te e - ter - na - men - te: fa - rò in -
Ev - 'ry window, you'll dis - cov - er, shall be tight-ly barr'd for ev - er!   I shall

cet - ta di chia - vac - ci, lucchet - ti - ni, luc - chet - ti - ni, ca - te -
buy me keys in plen-ty, Chains and padlocks, chains and padlocks ten or

Made in the USA
Las Vegas, NV
08 March 2021